INTERNET CONNECTE

I0018907

INTERNET CONNECTED WORLD

Author: Kambiz Mostofizadeh
Publisher: Mikazuki Publishing House
ISBN-13: 978-1-942825-06-7

INTERNET CONNECTED WORLD

INTRODUCTION

What will the future of business look like? Will humans still do their own shopping or will automated assistants shop for them? Will the Internet in the year 2050 be a place where all forms of discussion are honored or will the future of the Internet be one that disapproves of non-conformity? Will the Internet make my life easier other than allowing me to connect with friends? These are all questions that I have asked in this book. There is no correct or incorrect answer; rather it is my own judgements and opinions, gathered from extensive research, hands-on and academic, that I have conducted over the years. I encourage you to make your own decisions and to use critical thinking to arrive at what you believe the truth to be on any given matter. I only hope that you will enjoy my work and I hope that you will be kind enough to share it with others, so that they too can enjoy this book. Thank you for purchasing this book and I wish you the greatest of success in all your endeavors.

Sincerely,
Kambiz Mostofizadeh, Author

INTERNET CONNECTED WORLD

TABLE OF CONTENTS

INTERNET CONNECTED WORLD

HOLOGRAMS WILL DOMINATE PERFORMANCE ART

The use of holographic projectors to re-create performers will be a trend in the music and theatrical industries. Imagine the possibilities for a theatrical company that stages plays. Before the use of holograms, the theater company could only perform the play in one place. After the implementation of the hologram technology in the play, the play could be simultaneously performed on thousands of stages. What is a hologram? According to the Oxford Dictionaries, a hologram is a three-dimensional image formed by the interference of light beams from a laser or other coherent light source. In a theater play, the actors, actresses, set, background, and movement will be controlled by the holographic projector. Electrical engineer Dennis Gabor invented Holography or the science of making

INTERNET CONNECTED WORLD

holograms, in the late 1960's, for which he received a Nobel Prize in Physics in 1971. The use of holographic projectors have been used successfully in musical concerts to re-create musicians that are no longer and such use was able to generate and stimulate the public's attention. But the use of holograms will extend further in to the movie industry and in the future, popular movies will be made in a 3 dimensional format allowing the creation of the entire movie in to a hologram. In addition to viewing the movie in a flat screen format in a movie theater, the audience will now have the option to attend an open field and to watch the movie in a complete 3 dimensional manner. Instead of just viewing a flat screen, you will be able to walk around the scene 360 degrees and view it as if it were happening in front of you. This will stimulate greater interest to the movie industry because the audience will no longer feel passive but will now feel immersed in the scene. Additionally the use of hologram will extend areas such as security. Because security guards are used as deterrents to crime and not as active law enforcement, would it not be logical to use holograms to re-create the appearance of security? Extending this even further, it would not be illogical to see entire armies comprised of holograms defending vital areas. The holograms would project the appearance of strength and to a reconnaissance plane, this would not be any different than the real thing until its strength is tested. Holograms will also enter the sports industries and there will be entire sports leagues comprised of athlete holograms. The appearance of two hologram boxers fighting in front of an audience or home viewers would be no different than the real thing to the human eye. Imagine attending a basketball game

INTERNET CONNECTED WORLD

where a portion of the audience, the coaches, the players, and the cheerleaders are all holograms. This would increase revenues for sports team owners which is why sports team owners in the future will invest in holography. The use of holograms will dominate performance art in the future and will have many uses in scientific applications that have not yet been discovered.

 At one point, Myspace had over 40 billion page views per month.

INTERNET CONNECTED WORLD

TIME IS A CURRENCY

In the future, online marketplaces will broker time as a form of currency and individuals will provide their time to others in return for benefits. No money will be traded in this arrangement. It will be an online bartering arrangement in which millions of humans per day will provide services to each other for the purpose of lending their expertise to meet the need of another individual and in return receive services in compensation.

 The first website was made by Tim Berners-Lee.

Barter will be the main method of all future transactions and money will be of little value, as service trading becomes dominant. Every individual and every business on earth has a list of multiple services that they utilize in order

INTERNET CONNECTED WORLD

to satisfy the requirements of their business operations. No individual or business is able to operate in a vacuum, and the services they use are paid for in form of a salary to an individual or as an independent contractor to an individual or business. Certain services like bookkeeping, shipping, secretarial, marketing, sales, and others will always be needed regardless of the business model that is being used. The reason why many businesses are forced to pay for these services is because they have not been able to be matched with another business that would be able to both provide them the service and well as having a need that could be met by the company originally requesting the service. Through the use of Internet software, it would be relatively easy to match individuals and organizations together to be able to link the various required needs and to trade services without the need for financial compensation. Every service each company provides will have a visible financial value assigned to it so the balance, deficit or surplus, could be managed through that company's control panel or dashboard when they log in online. The values of the services could rise or fall in a stock market type fashion, based on the excess or lack of similar services in the online bartering marketplace. In essence, it is time that is being bartered. Time is the main currency in this online bartering marketplace and it is the time of an individual with a particular specialty that is lending their time/expertise in return to be compensated by an individual or business that is able to provide them with a service they are in need of. The future of online transactions will be through these online person to person marketplaces that will save potentially billions of dollars for the economies of nations that are able to effectively adopt it.

 AOL nearly bought Yahoo for around 5 million dollars.

3D PRINTED HOME OF THE FUTURE

The home of the future will be printed on a 3-D printer and assembled like toy building blocks. The home of the future will be assembled in under one week and will be done by a team of under 5 individuals. The home of the future will be planned by Computer Aided Drafting and then divided in to the thousands of pieces that need to be produced. Based on the sequential flow of the building construction, the pieces will be manufactured in the 3-D printer that is available at the construction site. The 3-D printer will most likely be the size of a 10 meter square room, allowing for the manufacturing of large parts items to be used in the house. The 3-D printer would be able to print all the items

 The home of the future will be manufactured and assembled in under a few days.

used in a house but the house of the future will differ in that it will use materials that can be easily used within the 3-D printer. For example, the printing of brick façade to be used on a home's exterior may be made of a special resin or plastic that is rust and decay resistant. The garage driveway flooring might be made of a similar material instead of being concrete. Strengthened high density plastic polymers could replace the use of wood and even in certain cases steel, for the use of columns. The foundation could also be printed in the 3-D printer in to various pieces and assembled in a

INTERNET CONNECTED WORLD

locking type format that would allow the rapid creation and assembly of a home's foundation, without the need for cement trucks and wasted time for drying. The roof of the home could easily be created in the 3-D printer as could the piping, saving vital time in building construction as well as eliminating any time that would have been wasted on sourcing and shipping the materials. Industrial size 3-D printers will be a common site at construction zones and their use will save vital construction funds that could be used for promoting the construction or that could be used in another area of the project which could add value to the end consumer. The 3-D printer will fundamentally change the way that the home of the future will be built and their use in home construction will be the rule and not the exception.

INTERNET CONNECTED WORLD

 The majority of humans on earth do not have access to the Internet.

CASE STUDY – AMERICA ONLINE (AOL)

It was the most important thing of my teens. Without it, life was just not as fun. It was really the best for chatting. That is what made me want to be on it and that is probably what attracted everyone to it. It was all about chat rooms and private messaging. It was the greatest thing ever. What started as the Control Video Corporation that featured boxes installed in your house to allow a virtual network, became the world's most famous online network. This was the first major social network and it owes its success to its former CEO Steve Case. Case was a master of building relationships and building private virtual social networks using the AOL model for customers such as Apple. Case spent months living in Palo Alto, California and even convinced the Apple folks to put a desk for him in the Customer Care center. Case, a Political Science degree holder (like myself), used his skills to play the various divisions of Apple against each other. Apple was a highly decentralized company at that time with each division making its own decisions. Case used this to his advantage and was able to convince

 AOL grew so large that it merged with Time-Warner.

the Customer Care department to start a initiative to start a private online network for Apple customers. Case fended off multiple takeovers from eccentric Steve Wozniack (who had amassed up to 20% of AOL stock at one time) but Case slipped in a "poison pill" clause in the Bylaws through the Board of Directors, that would make buying AOL prohibitively expensive for a company attempting a hostile takeover. Case kept immensely strenuous hours at AOL and he always compared keeping AOL alive to "maintaining a space shuttle indefinitely in space." Case spent most of his hours as the de-facto Mayor of AOL and spent much of his time exchanging emails and chatting online with customers. Case shined most during AOL's internet war with Microsoft that sought to decide who controlled the Internet Service Provider business in America. Case's input made AOL user friendly and hip, in comparison to Compuserve (a dinosaur) and Prodigy (too bookish). Case's only mistake came when he lead the takeover of Time Inc, one of the largest media corporations on earth.

INTERNET CONNECTED WORLD

Now AOL has been bought out by Verizon.
This is the way of corporations.

The Internet has over 1 billion web pages in it.

THE TURK AUTOMATON

The machine known as the Turk Automaton was invented by Hungarian nobleman Baron Wolfgang Von Kemplen in 1769. The Turk Automaton was a chess playing machine that was presented to and demonstrated for princes and potentates throughout Europe. The Turk

The Turk Automaton beat Napoleon in a game of Chess.

Automaton beat the best chess players in the world and even played against Napoleon

INTERNET CONNECTED WORLD

Bonaparte. Charles Babbage, the father of the modern computer, was inspired to create calculating machines because of it and the modern scientific and literary greats like Edgar Allen Poe wrote about its workings. Poe said "The Turk plays with his left hand. All the movements of the arm are at right angles. In this manner, the hand (which is gloved and bent in a natural way,) being brought directly above the piece to be moved, descends finally upon it, the fingers receiving it, in most cases, without difficulty. Occasionally, however, when the piece is not precisely in its proper situation, the Automaton fails in his attempt at seizing it. When this occurs, no second effort is made, but the arm continues its movement in the direction originally intended, precisely as if the piece were in the fingers." When it was demonstrated for the first time, individuals in attendance were in near shock as a machine

INTERNET CONNECTED WORLD

was able to beat the finest players in the world in Chess. Many theories were created about its workings and much writing was done

 Microsoft was founded in 1975.

speculating as to how it operated. Many believed that there was a man hidden inside the machine that allowed the machine to think and move the pieces. If this were so, the individual would have to have been a midget so as to be able to fit in to the machine. But even if this theory were true, where would you find a chess playing midget that was able to defeat the best chess players in the world? The other theory was that it was purely mechanical movements with the illusion of intelligence. The machine was mostly likely pure automata, an invention that was based around the movements of gears, wires, and pulleys. But the creation of a machine, at that time, was considered so fantasy-like that people were in near shock when witnessing it for the first time. If even it was purely a machine, how could a machine defeat the greatest chess players in Europe in the late 1700's? What advanced technologies were being used that allowed for this? The Turk Automaton was stored in a museum that burned down, destroying the machine forever. Imitations of the machine were created later but the original technology that Von Kemplen created was never seriously analyzed other than through observations of individuals watching the demonstrations. Von Kemplen was an extraordinary and gifted inventor of unusual creations. His Turk Automaton not only created a stir but also advanced the study of automata creation,

INTERNET CONNECTED WORLD

mostly importantly inspiring Charles Babbage's computing machines.

 The first website was made by Tim Berners-Lee.

THE FUTURE OF COMPUTERS

Imagine flipping through pictures on your computer just by moving your hand in the air from right to left. In future computers, all commands will be made by voice, by hand gestures in the mid-air, and by sounds. Similar to the computer that Tom Cruise was using in the film Minority Report, you too will flip through images and video while having your voice dictated as well as simultaneously recorded for later use. The future computer will be no larger than a softball, but it will project the screen, keyboard, and peripherals in the form of hologram. According to the Oxford University Press dictionary, a hologram is 'a three-dimensional image formed by the interference of light beams from a laser or other coherent light source'. The future computer will be super lightweight, portable, and intuitive. The ability to control it by voice command makes it easy to navigate. The

 Wikipedia has nearly 4 million English articles.

future computer will converse with you as well as assist in managing your life, freeing up your time. The future computer will also be able to communicate with your home automation system and will be able to give you updates on various items ranging from your home security, home temperature, which windows are open, your next appointment, or that you have guests

INTERNET CONNECTED WORLD

coming over. The future computer will be an assistant as well as a virtual friend. The future computer could also be controlled by brainwaves as well as eye movements. The fluctuations in the electrical activity of your brain allow for the creation of thoughts that would in turn be able to control the computer of the future. Also the addition of an eye tracking camera would control your motions and allow

 South Korea has the fastest Internet Connection speed in the world.

you to open files with just an eye movement. The future computer will be incomparable to the computers we are using today and their speed will be many times greater than current ones. The future computer will eventually shrink to a size no larger than a mobile phone but will have the power of a supercomputer.

INTERNET CONNECTED WORLD

With the intense focus by major firms on research and development, the new discoveries in computing technology will make the future computer the dream of every computer engineer.

 Twitter has over 300 million users.

INTERNET CONNECTED WORLD

FREEMIUM BUSINESS MODEL WORKS

Of all the various business models that are available to websites and online software, the freemium business model has been the most workable and financially advantageous one. This business model will dominate the future of e-business. The freemium business model allows for the free use of a site or software with the addition of having the user pay to access the premium features. It is a combination of the pay to use model and the free model. The advertising model has had mixed reviews from websites. Some websites have been wildly successful in attracting advertisers but for the most part, websites have struggled with creating a substantial advertising revenue channel. News websites like Wall Street Journal have been successful in using the subscription business model but that is owing more to the popularity of the brand and the loyalty that Wall Street Journal readers have for the brand. Most news websites operate on an advertising model and readers have for the most part been hesitant to pay for accessing news.

 The computer mouse was invented by Stanford Research Institute (SRI).

The advertising model, although not always successful for some sites, has still been able to generate a substantial amount of revenue for sites like newspapers that have been able to consistently generate new and fresh content. Sites like Facebook and Twitter that rely heavily on user generated content have been successful in attracting long term loyal advertisers but sites like The Drudge Report have relied on an advertising model. The decision as to what business model the site or software should use comes down to the price elasticity of the market in which the site or

 Cray Inc, the American supercomputer manufacturer, was founded in 1972.

software will be competing. As disposable incomes shrink and the amount of time available to individuals becomes less, having a product that can save individuals or corporations money will be the determining factor that defines whether a venture wins or fails. Additionally, the business model will be based specifically around the demographics and your target audience. The freemium model works because it gives the end user the best of both worlds. Also the site or software can commoditize certain parts of the site or software and allow the user to only pay for the modules or sections they are going to use. This empowers and enables the end user as well as creating loyalty for your brand.

 Michael Dell started his multi-billion dollar company from his college dorm room.

THE FUTURE OF RESTAURANTS

The future of restaurants lays in complete automation. You enter the restaurant and sit down at a 4 person booth. On the table at your booth is an LCD screen from where you order your food and pay for your food using digital currency. Once you have ordered, your order is sent to the kitchen where automated cooks prepare your food and place in to a metallic pot specially created for transporting the food and

INTERNET CONNECTED WORLD

keeping it warm. The metallic pot is placed on rails or tracks that have been installed

 McDonald's feeds over 48 million persons per day.

beforehand for the purpose of transporting the food to the restaurant patrons. After dining and leaving, the plates and forks are placed in to separate bins that automatically move the plates and forks to pre-arranged automated washing machines. Pure automation. The vision of the automated restaurant was created in the U.S. in the early 1950's as a solution to automate fast food burger restaurants. It was never implemented on a wide scale but it was tested on a local level. In a traditional restaurant, humans enjoy having their food served to them. Additionally, they enjoy interacting with restaurant employees. Over 12 percent of the entire U.S. labor force has worked for McDonald's at one point or another. The world's first fully automated restaurant known as Baggers has opened in Germany. The restaurant has enjoyed great success and patrons have been enthralled by the novelty aspect of it. For a fast food restaurant, which is essentially a mini-factory, automation may be a financial boon as prices of raw food materials rise and labor shortages become a reality. All restaurants in the future will feature automation in one form or another, whether it is order automation, food preparation automation, or food delivery automation. If major companies like Amazon can deliver packages by drones, is it a stretch of the imagination to think that multi-billion dollar food corporations will utilize drones to deliver your food to your house?

INTERNET CONNECTED WORLD

 Drones will deliver your food to your home in the future.

PRODUCTS DIVIDE

You never grow accustomed to hearing the horribly cliché terms in business like "one stop shop" or "one solution". There is no such thing as the one solution. Products and product categories divide rather than converge. What about the mobile phone? It is a now a device that claims to be able to do thousands of things. But ultimately, when you want to make a phone call, you use your mobile as a phone. You can use a mobile phone as a computer just like you can use aluminum foil as a sunshade for your car. But is aluminum foil the ideal sunshade for your car? Of course not and neither is the mobile phone effective as a computer. I cannot write this article with ease on a mobile phone. I cannot comfortably create spreadsheets on my mobile phone. Remember the convergence of the telephone and fax machine? It neither worked well as a fax machine nor worked well as a phone. If you are

 In the future, the majority of Grocery Shopping will be done online.

in need of brain surgery, do you choose a brain surgeon or do you choose a general medical practitioner? You would of course wisely choose the brain surgeon because the brain surgeon has specialization and expertise in that field. What if you met an individual and they told you they are a Doctor, Lawyer, Architect, Athlete, and Plumber, all in one. You would think that individual is probably lying and even if they are not lying, you would not use them for what you need to get done because they are lacking in specialization. An individual that has a broad knowledge of everything is lacking in specialization. Every human you meet on a daily basis or have met in your life, you categorize. That person is a Lawyer. That

 In Norway, all prisoners have access to the Internet.

person is an Architect. That person is a Writer. We classify humans in to categories and recall that information based on our need at that time. This categorization is automatic and allows us to operate more efficiently. If the joining together or convergence of products had any use, then you would be calling your friend from your Television and warming up

INTERNET CONNECTED WORLD

your food in the built in microwave in your refrigerator. But after years of realizing that product convergence does not work, this has not stopped executives of major tech companies from continuing to sell you this fable. Major Japanese conglomerates learned all too well the problems with doing everything. Profit margins shrank to nearly zero. But specialists enjoy high profit margins and they have the legitimacy and expertise to operate in their respective fields.

 Nearly half of all Internet traffic is non-human.

INTERNET CONNECTED WORLD

MAJORITY OF ONLINE TRAFFIC IS STREAMING

The majority of online data use is streaming, as Internet users listen to music and watch videos online. There are various reports from researchers claiming that up to 3/4th of Internet users actively stream music and watch films online. For some individuals, watching television online is more important than using other mediums such as cable and satellite. Major online movie distributors like Netflix, Amazon, Hulu, and others are responsible for streaming movies and documentaries to online viewers. The use of the Internet to stream music and video became commonplace as Internet usage began to overtake the television as the main entertainment piece of the household. The rapid streaming speed available to Internet users have enabled them to switch from a TV centered approach for

INTERNET CONNECTED WORLD

viewing films to an Internet centered approach for viewing films.

 The Internet's use grew faster than the Radio.

The medium has had mixed reviews from film production houses that are cautious about licensing the rights to their films without royalties or a substantial licensing arrangement. Streaming music providers like Pandora, Spotify, Rhapsody, and others have made a huge impact in the way that music fans access their favorite music or find new music. In addition, YouTube has also released a music service after discovering that a large portion of their streaming content being accessed by users is music videos. The

INTERNET CONNECTED WORLD

 MTV created the category of music television broadcasting.

streaming services for music and video have made up the bulk of Internet traffic but there is much room for improvement as Internet speeds rise. Areas that can be improved on include online traffic management and increasing streaming speeds. The higher the speeds that are available, the greater options that are available to programmers when building online software. Online traffic will make up the bulk of Internet use for the foreseeable future and will grow as the usage of the Internet to stream music and video overtakes the use of the television. Additionally, because the majority of humans on earth do not yet have access to the Internet, the future of streaming music and video cannot

INTERNET CONNECTED WORLD

be predicted accurately. With the reduction of international poverty and the increase in Internet usage, streaming music and video could eventually make up to ninety percent of all Internet data traffic.

 By 2050, all digital devices will be able to communicate and sync.

INTERNET CONNECTED TOYS

The merging of the Internet and toys is a perfect match and it is one that was set to happen. Toys like dolls that are connected to the Internet, allow for play un-like that which has been seen before. Internet connected toys can do such things as take pictures that can be stored online or shared online. But what happens when Internet connected toys get a computer virus? What happens when Internet

INTERNET CONNECTED WORLD

connected toys are hacked in to and your private online files have been accessed? The Internet is a vast ocean of computers talking to each other. As Internet users, we have to know what information can be stored online and we should make an intelligent decision as to what we should store online. Just because you are behind a computer screen does not mean you are not accountable for your thoughts, words, and actions. You should not develop a false sense of safety behind the computer screen whether you are or whether you are not committing an illegal act. Hackers target many websites for various reasons, ranging from political to economic. But because there has been one or two incidences where hackers have accessed Internet connected toys, does not mean that they are un-safe. What it does mean is that gaps in online security have now been identified and these gaps and

INTERNET CONNECTED WORLD

 By 2050, all Internet users will be assigned a recognizable Internet ID upon birth, to prevent identity theft and fraud.

vulnerabilities will now be closed to future hackers. When a hacker uses Denial of Service (dos) or other hacks to access a site, now the hacker or hackers have just revealed that they exist. Now their hand has been revealed and they will be the one that is now a fugitive from law enforcement. The website that was hacked will just continue operating and will now address the vulnerabilities that exist in the system. Internet connected toys are as safe as laptops, desktop computers, tablets, and mobile phones that access the Internet. They can all be hacked so it's completely un-fair to single out Internet connected toys as being un-safe. Internet connected toys are hardware

INTERNET CONNECTED WORLD

devices in the form of functional art that use software to do an assortment of things to entertain including taking pictures, recording audio, and using Text To Speech (TTS) to communicate. Internet connected toys are the future and the future is now.

The World Wide Web (WWW) was created in Switzerland.

INTERNET CONNECTED WORLD

THE FUTURE OF ADVERTISING

As a former media buyer that was responsible for purchasing up to $500,000 of media space per month, I have witnessed the Internet advertising industry evolve and change. What used to be an industry that revolved around CPM or Cost Per Thousand views switched to a CPC or Cost Per Click model, that favors advertisers. Advertisers began to demand greater transparency and targeting capabilities to be able to reach relevant users of their

 By 2050, advertising will be tailored personally for you.

products or services. Traditional television has been the main avenue for advertisers to reach their potential markets. With the advent of the Internet, TV use had dropped as mobile phones and laptops took dominance. Why did

INTERNET CONNECTED WORLD

the Internet cause TV use to drop? Internet users like having the ability to choose what they would like to watch rather than having what they watched pre-programmed for them. This enabled and empowered Internet users to give priority to content that satisfied them greater. Measurement tools took priority as the analysis and statistics generated by advertising was honed to a science. The future of advertising will continue to use measurement in multiple forms, especially in the video sector.

 By 2050, Electronic Money will become the norm in all online and offline transactions.

The main problem with advertising on online video is that individuals can do the same thing that they did when they watched offline video, and that is to mute the advertisement. What will the video advertiser with all his measurement tools achieve when the viewer simply mutes the video? The future of advertising has not yet been defined in an evolving industry. Online advertising, outdoor advertising, and transit advertising (advertising on trains, cars, etc.) are all in evolution. Radio in many cases has been more effective than television in being able to reach potential customers. Transit advertising has also been in many cases more effective than offline and online television advertising. Why would this be? The reason is that an individual sitting in a train or an individual sitting in a car is captive and will have no choice to listen or view the advertisement. But a person watching online and offline video can simply mute the audio, negating the advertiser's hopes of having a successful advertising campaign. As the future of the advertising industry is a work in progress, new technologies will become available that will allow both measurement and effective penetration.

 A truly new product means that a new category of product has been created.

ROLE OF VISION IN PRODUCT DEVELOPMENT

There is an ongoing problem occurring in large and small corporations, whether member run or board run. The problem revolves around a lack of vision in product development. Of course larger companies take longer to make decisions and have to expend much more resources in contrast to smaller companies.

INTERNET CONNECTED WORLD

 Lack of vision in product development leads to creation of mediocre products. But smaller companies will always maintain the advantage of rapidity. Additionally, larger companies, despite vast resources, are not guaranteed by any means to achieve success in a product category that they are not specialized in. Products are developed for today but by the time the product is actually developed and ready for marketing, the product becomes deficient. The mobile phone manufacturing industry has experienced this problem as has the fashion industry. Fads are short term but trends are long term. Although trends are long term, this does not mean that the trend will benefit you, only that the trend will continue to exist. Trends move upward and move downward. Companies develop products to meet the current demand and rarely do

companies create products without there being a "critical mass" of buyers available for that market. The company enters the market only to discover their competitors have already launched a better product. What is the solution to creating products that will meet a current or future demand?

Smaller organizations can make faster decisions.

An intelligent approach to product development would be to identify a product category in which their will be a new sub-category created and to create a product now for that future market category. What happens when a me-too product enters a category? Ask Richard Branson and the Virgin Cola brand what happened when he entered the soft drinks category. You can't fight an uphill battle and you won't gain traction by pushing a boulder up a steep hillside. That is where vision steps in and creates an atmosphere of innovation that allows for the creation of a new product that is both useful and fresh. Too many managers are stuck in far off offices with plans and decisions made by committee. The best products in history were created by the vision of a single individual that believed that he or she could make a change. Have vision.

 Don't waste resources on a product that is just a better version of your competitor's.

INTERNET CONNECTED WORLD

IS TIME TRAVEL POSSIBLE?

It would be the dream of many individuals to travel back in to the past to visit a loved one or even to engage in thoughtful discussion with an important figure in history. Is time travel possible? According to English Physicist Brian Cox, time travel is theoretically possible, but the individual would only be able to travel in to the future and not to the past. In the early 1960's mathematician Roy Kerr proposed a theory that argued that black holes could be used to enter an alternative universe. Black holes are created by the collapsing of a star and the gravitational field that is generated within it and around it. Professor Cox argued in a presentation at the 2013 British Science Festival, that a wormhole could be used to travel in to the future. According to City University of New York astrophysicist Charles

INTERNET CONNECTED WORLD

Liu, you can travel forward in the future by way of the 4th dimension known as 'space-time'.

 Time travel could create a Parallel Universe where two of you exist at the same time.

A wormhole is essentially a shortcut that allows you to move to forward in time. There are many issues with time travel that can only be solved as of now in theory. For example, what if you travel forward in time, say 25 years to visit your future grandchildren. You would, according to Quantum Theory, exist both in the future and in the present, which would mean there would be two of you now. Your time travel would create a parallel universe. Additionally, if you adjust or try to change your future, there may be a chance that it would affect your past. Commercial and practical applications of time travel could be developed to use the technology to instantly transport products to far distances, such as sending vital items to disaster stricken areas. According to Einstein's theory of General Relativity, an astronaut traveling at the speed of light would feel the effects of aging as a period of a few

 By 2050, Time Travel technology will be used for shipping purposes.

years whereas over 50 will have gone by on planet earth. The CERN Institute's Large Hadron Collider in Switzerland could be the only particle collider machine capable of re-creating a small wormhole. China has announced that it will be building a particle accelerator 7 times more powerful and twice the size of CERN's Large Hadron Collider. The possibilities of time travel will continue to interest physicists and various scientists alike as China and CERN continue their experiments.

HOW CAN WE CLEAN THE EARTH?

Carbon emissions are a major cause of greenhouse gases that deplete the ozone layer which protects us from the sun's harmful UV rays. How can we clean the earth? Regulation causes corporations to feel they are being restricted and/or are lacking freedom in carrying out certain operations. But without top-down regulation, there would be nothing to stop individuals and corporations from coincidentally destroying local environments and habitats while attempting to produce profits. Cleaning the earth will unfortunately take more than top-down approaches.

INTERNET CONNECTED WORLD

 Pollution destroys the environment and causes natural habitats to be destroyed.

If the earth is to be cleaned by 2050, it is to start today from the ground level, and that means individuals will have to take steps to ensure that their children and grandchildren will have a clean environment to live in. Of course, pre-emptive steps can be taken to ensure such and they include switching to renewable energy sources and reducing use of fossil fuels. At the individual level, persons could wear a portable air cleaner/air ionizer (negative ion generator), that would be able to clean the area around the person in a one meter radius. This portable air cleaner would be able to clean the area around the individual, allowing them to breathe clean air while being able to produce excess clean air to add to the environment around them.

 By 2050, all vehicles will be zero emissions, meaning they will emit zero harmful gases.

Through the ionization of air particles, air ionization devices depending on their Clean Air Delivery Rate (CADR), could be a vital boon to metropolitan areas with populations of over 15,000,000. An inexpensive portable wearable air ionizer would make every person wearing one a walking mobile air cleaner and through its mass use, there could be a substantial change in a city's air quality. Larger versions of the air ionization device, the size of a 3 meter statue, could be created to be put in to all neighborhoods in a city, with parks being an ideal location for their installation and use. Whether air ionizers are made and used in

INTERNET CONNECTED WORLD

portable wearable sizes or if they are made in the shape of towers to be installed in local areas, their widespread use could have a worthwhile impact for the future of the earth.

 Keep the earth clean. There is only one earth so protect it.

INTERNET CONNECTED WORLD

CAN THE INTERNET SAVE THE ENVIRONMENT BY 2050?

The Internet has made huge strides in multiple sectors by being able to optimize the efficiency and productivity of their industries. There have been numerous environmentally focused sites that have been created in the past years that have aimed to reduce carbon emissions or that have sought to raise funds for the protection of the environment. Internet users are (for the most part) environmentally conscious individuals and many Internet-based initiatives that have sought to gather support for eco-projects have been successful. Millionaire Johan Eliasch created a trust that purchased 400,000 acres of Amazonian rainforest from a logging company in Brazil. His example has helped to influence other entrepreneurs. 160 acres of forest land are destroyed per minute due to deforestation. The amount of venture

INTERNET CONNECTED WORLD

capitalists seeking to invest in green companies or companies that invest in renewable energy sources (solar, wind, etc.) have steadily increased.

 By 2050, Environmental Cleaning Robots will be commonplace in factories & worksites.

In addition, there has been a trend in crowdfunding eco-based projects that seek to acquire areas for preservation. Internet based marketplaces for trading carbon emissions have become a reality, though its impact and breadth of activity has not reached its optimal state.

 Deforestation destroys over 1,000 acres per minute.

INTERNET CONNECTED WORLD

The Internet can and does perform as an Early Warning System (EWS) than can reveal areas of the earth that are facing environmental damage. A centrally located EWS would allow people with Internet access, from various parts of the world to share and coordinate information that could be correlated to create "a bigger picture" as to the scale of the damage the earth is sustaining. The use of the Internet to save the environment is a relatively new trend, but it is a trend that will continue to gather supporters and wield the power to influence the environmentally conscious beliefs of all Internet users. As the Internet is still in its infancy, the growth of the Internet environmental movement will be rapid as Internet users seek to show their solidarity with the protection of the environment.

INTERNET CONNECTED WORLD

 The sun is the cleanest source of energy that exists.

DREAMS OF SOLAR NOT REACHED

Besides major advances in solar energy devices and photovoltaic cells (energy storing solar cells), the true dream of solar energy has not yet been realized. Solar technology has been implemented for some devices such as home water heaters or are being used to assist in the generation of energy alongside standard electricity utility service, but have not created an all-encompassing presence in our lives. The use of photovoltaic cells have been centered on providing energy for single family homes. Photovoltaic cells have not yet impacted our lives because the use of photovoltaic cells have not yet been implemented in everyday appliances and devices. Your mobile phone should be solar powered. Your car should be solar powered. Is there any reason your car should be able to drive 200 kilometers per hour? Unless you are a race car driver in a racing contest featuring spectators, you should not be driving speeds that can result in catastrophic accidents.

 By 2050, Solar will be the number one energy source for home energy consumption.

Motorcycles emit far more carbon emissions in comparison to automobiles. The use of solar energy to power motorcycles and scooters will greatly reduce carbon emissions in major urban centers that feature populations of over 12,000,000. Solar is self-sustaining and a clean renewable source of energy. Your laptop or tablet computer should be solar powered. In addition, you should have a solar powered

INTERNET CONNECTED WORLD

scanner and solar powered printer, so that you can always scan and print your files without the need for plugging in to outlets and implementing mechanisms for power conversion. Kitchen appliances should also be solar powered as well because most kitchens have an ample supply of sunlight available to them. Cars, motorcycles, mobile phones, laptops, tablets, scanners, printers, and kitchen appliances should all be solar powered. In addition, portable power packs that store energy should also be solar powered. The use of photovoltaic cells should infiltrate all sectors of manufacturing and its implementation should be a priority rather than an afterthought.

 By 2050, Computer Aided Surgery (CAS) will be the main tool for hospital surgeons.

INTERNET CONNECTED WORLD

AN ADVANCED MEDICAL FUTURE

Imagine being able to provide first responder medical service instantly without the need for a medical professional to be present. The future of the Internet and the Internet of Things (IOT) will include every home having a medical device that is hooked up to their laptop, tablet, mobile phone, or home computer. The device will be a4 sized (8.5 x 11 inches) and will provide instant testing with a print out in a report form. The device will feature an LED screen and will have WIFI capability. The medical device will allow pregnancy testing, HIV testing, blood pressure testing, blood oxygen level testing, and various medical tests. The medical device will also manage the patient's pill delivery, prescriptions, and medical appointments. The medical device will be voice controlled and will have an artificial intelligence system. Depending on pre-

INTERNET CONNECTED WORLD

assigned parameters in the various tests, a Doctor or even an ambulance service may be notified. In many cases, the various routine tests are run on the medical device and the "patient" will have instant information provided to them.

In addition, the medical device's artificial intelligence will give you simple medical advice or even automatically make an appointment with a medical professional for further examination. The benefits of the medical device are many, but firstly it will reduce the pressure placed on the medical system for routine tests that could be conducted "in-house".

 By 2050, medical results will be available instantly to the patient.

INTERNET CONNECTED WORLD

The savings in the first year alone would be in the hundreds of millions of dollars. In addition, the medical device would contact your Pharmacist, coordinate prescription paperwork and schedule a delivery to fill your prescriptions.

Two sizes of the medical device could be released, one a4 sized and one vending machine sized. The vending machine sized could provide the medical services for an apartment complex.

 By 2050, Custom Medicine will be developed for you based on your DNA.

The a4 sized medical device would be a personal portable device that could be transported easily with the patient. The future will feature advanced medical devices that will make medical services more accessible, less expensive, and more convenient.

By 2050, up to 25 percent of all nurses will be robots.

CASE STUDY (BUSINESS)
WHAT I LEARNED FROM GETTY

J Paul Getty was one of the first American billionaires and he made his fortune in oil exploration, working as a "wildcatter" in the Ozarks. Getty believed that overhead costs are a mere illusion, used only as cosmetic dressing to project an image of success. Getty signed all his oil contracts on the hood of his "Tin Lizzie" aka Model-T Ford. At the height of Getty's wealth, all his international oil ventures that generated tens of billions of dollars were run from a modest 5 story building that held no more than 100 people. Getty believed that an efficient and organized team could have synergistic effects which would act as a force multiplier, giving an organization a distinct advantage over its competitors. Getty believed in being hands-on and setting an example for everyone in his organization. Although it may have been difficult for him to execute many of his policies for personal reasons, he showed discipline in practicing the same as he extolled his employees to do. Getty believed that as a business owner or as a manager, you cannot

 J. Paul Getty's Father got rich from inventing a new type of self-sharpening oil drilling bit.

expect your employees to work harder than you. Getty believed that the owner of the company should work harder than his employees and be a positive example from which employees can gain motivation and inspiration. Getty argued that if you tell your employee to show up at 7:30am, you should show up earlier, for example 7am. Getty having himself worked as a roughneck on an oil rig (a physically demanding job), believed in leading from the front, not barking orders from the back. Getty also believed that you should not invest in a business that you cannot directly control. Getty's business philosophies were unique and the best business according to Getty is the business that you control, but own no stake in. Getty also argued for the creation of a Federal Department in the U.S. that would fund the art. Getty argued that a sophisticated man is a man that loves art, theater, and music.

INTERNET CONNECTED WORLD

 J. Paul Getty believed in leading from the front and being "hands-on".

Getty believed that the downfall of society (the creation of the un-sophisticated person) stems from its lack of appreciation for art. Getty also believed that the employees should be rewarded according to performance (bonuses) and their annual salary should be adjusted to reflect the company's strong or weak performance. Getty's unique business philosophies have inspired countless titans of industry and has provided a model for success.

 Getty would arrive at work at least 30 minutes to one hour before his employees.

INTERNET CONNECTED WORLD

CASE STUDY (BUSINESS)
WHAT I LEARNED FROM HERSHEY

The frugal Dutchman went bankrupt 7 times before becoming a success but he never gave up his determination to win. His success wasn't Hershey chocolate as that came after his success with selling caramels for a penny a piece. His success with caramels funded Hershey Chocolate Bars that were priced at a nickel in the early 1900's. His success from his caramels funded the construction and development of a rural township in to a city called Hershey, Pennsylvania. Before he was 60 years old, he gave away ALL his riches to a Trust that still exists today.

 Hershey built a city in Pennsylvania.

INTERNET CONNECTED WORLD

This Trust created the Hershey School that funds thousands of students every year from around the U.S. Having lost his Irish-American wife Kitty to illness and not having children inspired Hershey to create the Hershey School. These students live in Hershey, Pennsylvania at the school dorms, receiving a first rate education at the expense of the Hershey Trust. In fact, it is this Trust that controls the Hershey company, not the other way around. When he was older and retired, he opened a store on the Atlantic City boardwalk selling Hershey soaps.

Hershey had become obsessed with soap manufacturing in his retirement and his soap became a small hit with New York hotels, until one of the patrons of the Waldorf Astoria thought the soap was chocolate and ate it. Hershey's life taught me that success has no monetary figure. Success is about achieving not about earning money. Hershey kept achieving despite his many setbacks and

 Hershey was an empire builder and a visionary.

failures and this eventually lead to his success. Hershey's life also taught me that you must risk all to win all. If you want to win you have to be 100% determined to win with every available resource at your disposable. Hershey invested nearly everything he had in the creation of Hershey, Pennsylvania and was rewarded greatly for his vision. Sales volume is more important than high profit margins. Hershey chocolates consistently sold because they offered more chocolate in their bars at a lower price than their competitors. Hershey's life also taught me that money should be used for greater purposes than self-indulgence. Hershey gave away nearly everything he had before the age of 60.

 Hershey Bars were originally 5 cents apiece.

He did this to fund the Hershey School that provided a first class education to thousands from across the U.S. Hershey's life also taught me that you have to know as much or more than your employees. Hershey was a hands-on leader and spent much of his time experimenting to create new milk chocolate bars and confectionaries.

INTERNET CONNECTED WORLD

 A business model should be well planned and polished before being executed.

WHY START-UPS WILL STILL FAIL IN 2050

Why are some start-ups successful and why do some start-up companies fail? A start-up company seeks to grow to become a "unicorn" or a start-up whose valuation is worth more than $1,000,000,000. Start-ups share similar starts but there trajectory changes due to several factors including business model, future value of target market, leadership style, type, and their solvency. The Internet has featured scores of failed start-ups that featured an unworkable or un-profitable business model.

INTERNET CONNECTED WORLD

 Milton Hershey spent most of his time in Research & Development.

Many of the first Internet start-ups had their business plans and related business model scribbled out on a napkin. Venture capitalists were quick to put their funds in to anything Internet related but quickly learned that not all business models are equal. Failed start-ups featured business models that spent more in customer acquisition costs than generated revenue. The Future Value of a Target Market (FVTM) cannot always be calculated. Many start-ups found success in a trial and error manner because the market they were seeking to dominate did not exist. The start-ups were founded to create a product when the "critical mass" of buyers did not exist to justify a venture capital investment.

INTERNET CONNECTED WORLD

 A "unicorn" is a start-up whose valuation is worth more than $1,000,000,000.

Customer acquisition costs are obligatory especially when the market must be created for the product. The leadership style of the start-up will determine their future success. A disruptive type of start-up can reap great benefits as start-up Uber has experienced. Complimentary types of start-ups are also successful because they act as enablers for that specific industry. Solvency has always been a goal for all start-ups.

 High cash burn rates with little income generation, leads to the downfall of businesses.

INTERNET CONNECTED WORLD

Start-ups have high cash burn rates causing their venture capital funders anxiety. The faster that a start-up reaches solvency, the sooner the shareholders can be rewarded for their investment. Too many Internet start-ups had to shut down operations because their revenue could not match their intensively high cash burn rate. Spending vital funds on items that do not add value to the customer is not intelligent and burns through a start-up's reserves. By viewing factors such as a start-up's business model, future value of target market, leadership style, type, and their solvency, a venture capitalist will better understand if that start-up is a viable investment.

INTERNET CONNECTED WORLD

UX DESIGNS OF THE FUTURE

UX Design or User Experience Design is the study and application of User Interface design

 The best UX Design is the one that is most user friendly.

methods that seek to maximize the customer experience. UX design involves multiple principles and they include flexibility, usability, simplicity, and scalability (FUSS). FUSS principles allow for the creation of UX that is pleasurable for the end consumer and is designed around maximizing the experience that the user undergoes during use of the software or website. The UX Designer using the FUSS principles can create an experience that is both simple and effective for the end user. The flexibility allows for future changes in the design, usability allows for a fast learning curve and empowers users to have control, simplicity allows for clarity and reduces extra steps, and scalability allows for the ability to maintain optimum performance if the amount of

The most important feature of UX Design is Usability.

users are increased. The UX Designer uses the principles of Ergonomics or the science of maximizing use and performance. In addition, the human-system interaction is a customer centered design that involves the participation of the user during and after the design. Usability is at the forefront of UX design because it seeks to optimize the effectiveness and satisfaction of the user's experience. The user's experience is gauged during interaction with the interactive system known as the User Interface or UI. The first question that a UX Designer should ask is "Who is the end user and what goals are they seeking to achieve?"

The customer knows more about your product, than you do.

A customer centered approach will yield the most results during UX Design because the UI can be optimized or changed entirely to fit the needs of the system's user. Wireframing and prototyping are two tools that a UX Designer will utilize to achieve a rough draft of their design. Wireframing are the plans for your software or website, and they show the visual placement of the elements of your software as well as their context. Wireframing allows for the proper planning of the design and reveals the elements that are missing, those that need revising, and elements that need removing.

 The customer approach should be taken to UX Design.

Without wireframing, software would be poorly built, inefficiently designed, and the application of the FUSS principles would be sporadic at best. Rapid prototyping is also useful and can be an additional tool to static prototyping. Based on the complexity of the software, rapid prototyping may even be needed to allow for the viewing of a working mock-up. In contrast to wireframing that leaves out the graphical design elements, rapid prototyping provides a simple but useful tool that provides content architecture and communication layer elements in to it.

INTERNET CONNECTED WORLD

 The less people
involved in the
design, the
smoother the design
process will be.

NEURAL NETWORKS WILL DOMINATE

FUTURE COMPUTING

Neural networks are computing systems that

use hardware and software to make complex

decisions. The characteristics of neural

networks include the ability to learn and it is the

learning process that allows the neural network

 Neural Networks
are connected
computers that use
AI to seemingly
learn.

to increase in efficiency. Neural networks are

inspired by the learning ability, structure, and

processing method of the human brain. The

current commercial applications include (but are not limited to) speech recognition, handwriting recognition, data processing, robotics, and are even used for filtering spam email. Neural networks are expressive models that contain multiple non-linear hidden layers. Neural networks feature distributed representation so that information is stored in separate components, allowing them to be retrieved by their content. In addition, neural networks are fault tolerant, which allows the neural network to still continue working despite a failure in one part of the system. Neural networks are able to output faster decisions because they are dependent on parallel computing, that uses multiple processors (computers) to simultaneously process data. Neural networks are expensive systems that empower, for example, an insurance company to be able to make a complex decision like that of insuring a customer, by providing the necessary inputs through a feed forward system. This allows for the neural network to make correlations in the data and to organize that information in to each relevant category.

 By 2050, the majority of commercial transactions will be conducted by Neural Networks.

Every input pattern that is sent in to the neural network will provide an answer based on the pre-assigned algorithm. Neural networks are effective tools for prediction and forecasting, categorization, and pattern recognition and classification. A large number of inputs feed information in to the hidden layers that compute the information and relay that to the output(s). Neural networks use varying modes of learning whether supervised or un-

INTERNET CONNECTED WORLD

supervised, using multiple nodes (units) to attempt to copy the natural biological decision making process of the human brain. As computing power increases, the use of neural networks will be commonplace in the majority of industries.

 By 2050, Internet Privacy will be 100 percent controlled by users rather than websites.

INTERNET CONNECTED WORLD

INTERNET PRIVACY IN 2050

What is Internet Privacy (IP) and how does it affect us as Internet users? IP is the section of data privacy that deals with how your personal information is managed by websites that you use. IP lays down the rules for Internet users so they are aware how their information is being used and where it is being stored. Because the user's information is stored on the server of the website they are using, the website bears ultimate responsibility for maintaining the security of that information. For example, in the case of a social networking website like Facebook, users are able to download a PDF of their information, including their posts. Changes in the Terms of Service (TOS) or the Privacy Policy can cause users to stop using or reduce the amount of time they will be using a website. By 2050, users will have the ability to stop a website from changing its Privacy Policy without majority consent of its users.

Websites that store a user's information should provide a mechanism for the user to not only download their information, but also to delete their information. Websites that store a user's information but are unable to provide these two simple tools for empowering user's with their own information, should be avoided. Websites use database technology (MySQL, etc.) to store a user's information therefore enabling users to access their own information.

 By 2050, every human on earth will have a Social Media profile in one form or another.

By being able to access their own information, users feel more comfortable using that website. A website that does not allow you to delete

INTERNET CONNECTED WORLD

your own picture is a website that is not empowering the user. In addition, every time that a website wants to make a change to an item in the Terms of Service or in the Privacy Policy, every user should be notified via multiple channels. This ensures every user has the ability to have knowledge of the change, making the change both fair and open. The use of a user's information by third parties additionally has to be given approval by the users. By the user agreeing to give third party partners of the website access to their information, they will receive most likely advertising messages and offers for products. The approval should not be a blanket approval or an all-encompassing approval, but should rather be an open system that lists the third parties that approvals are sought for. If in the case that a third party's website is hacked or if the website that is storing the information gets hacked, the responsibility and accountability lies with the website owner. Before a website is created that stores users information, a Privacy Policy should be created, to allow for a clear roadmap that assists in the creation of the website, taking in to consideration the role of all users.

 By 2050, law enforcement will begin to utilize robots for information gathering.

ROBOTICS HOPE HAS EXCEEDED REALITY

Looking back at predictions from the early 1970's regarding the year 2000, you would think that commercially usable robot technology would be widely available. The predictions have hardly materialized, but the

INTERNET CONNECTED WORLD

hope that technology will match the pace of scientific vision, will continue. Robotic vacuums have been readily available for at least a decade. Robotic technology has barely begun to enter the toy industry, with animatronics being used to simulate animals and humans. Personal drones are available that allow you to film a gathering with a capability that would have previously cost tens of thousands of dollars and was only available to the film industry. In Japan, robotic 'nurses' are used to deliver items to patients. Robotics is widely used by leading corporations for manufacturing.

 By 2050, the majority of Industrial Manufacturing jobs will be given to robots.

Robots are being currently marketed to factories that act as security guards that register video and sound in real time while transmitting that information via WIFI to an internal server. Japanese researchers have pioneered research on artificial intelligence engines and life like androids. Androids are created to act and look like real humans, which make them an excellent addition to theme parks, acting as part of an attraction. The use

 By 2050, the use of Robot Security Guards for personal safety will be legalized.

of robotics, whether in industrial applications, as androids, as nurses, or as drones, have barely scratched the surface in the uses that are derived from robots. By the year 2050, robotics will begin to dominate all laborious activities and will even make themselves present in commercial activities, include purchasing and sales. Medicine will also benefit greatly from robotics. For example, a pet robot could be created that would be used specifically to stimulate conversation in individuals above the age of 65, reducing their risk of memory loss. Robots could also be used as mobile hospitals, arriving at a patient's house and administering medical tests and transmitting that information in real time to a Doctor, who could decide whether the patient would need specialized care.

 The use of robotics in manufacturing will reduce job accidents to zero.

Robots could also be used to clean environmental disasters, reducing the risk to human labor. The amount of labor saving tasks that could be thought of are countless, but the reality remains that our hopes for advanced

INTERNET CONNECTED WORLD

technological growth have far exceeded the research and development required to reach it.

A FUTURE INTERNET OF THINGS

The "Internet Of Things" or IOT are the "things" or physical devices that are connected to the Internet. The IOT includes, but is not limited to, laptops, tablets, mobile phones, desktop computers, smart watches, smart shoes, and smart clothing. Desktops were the traditional tool for computing but were replaced by laptops, which feature less bulkiness with equal functionality.

 By 2050, a new communication standard will be created that will be able to connect all hardware devices.

INTERNET CONNECTED WORLD

Tablets and mobile phones began to replace laptop use for consumer (not business) use. The future IOT will feature individuals wearing smart clothing that measures the user's temperature, gauge the user's heart rate, and contain a cooling/heating system that can instantly adjust itself based on the user's temperature. The smart clothing will be WIFI enabled and be able to send and receive information with the user's smart shoes, smart watch, and mobile phone. The user's smart shoes will measure the amount of steps in Kilometers and maintain a record of that information on the solid state hard disk within the shoes.

 By 2050, all clothing will be "Smart Clothing" with reporting ability.

INTERNET CONNECTED WORLD

The shoes will broadcast the information via Bluetooth technology, WIFI, or via USB cable to any computing device, whether portable (mobile phone, tablet, laptop) or cloud based (storage system). The user's smart watch will function as more than a time telling device or simple messaging device, providing management over the smart clothing and smart shoes, providing constant updates to the user's mobile phone. The integration of various devices will make the Internet Of Things be able to work together to create new abilities. Distributed computing projects like that used by SETI, have 3 million users that have downloaded a program on to their computers. These 3 million computers are running a program that uses their computing

 Chinese is the number one language on the Internet.

INTERNET CONNECTED WORLD

power to analyze data from telescopes. The future IOT will feature distributed computing applications that can utilize the power of millions of devices and use them collectively with one organized system.

One Internet user, whether on a mobile phone, laptop, tablet, or desktop, will have the capability of one million Internet users combined. The Internet is evolving and will continue evolving as long as it will exist. It is a network of computers that allow for communication between its users. United States, Europe, and UK quickly established their dominance in the Internet sector. With roughly 500 million Internet users combined in the U.S., European Union, and U.K., this is half of the 1 billion Internet users in Brazil, Russia, India, and China.

INTERNET CONNECTED WORLD

 By 2050, there will be more hardware devices made per year than there are humans on earth. China as of 2015 is the world's largest economy and Chinese is the most widely spoken language on the Internet. India and the United States are nearly equal in the amount of Internet users. Asian Internet powerhouses are beginning to flex their digital muscle and have been successful in crossing over in to foreign markets, launching financially favorable IPO's. The Internet will continue to change as the cross-cultural divides are bridged allowing for International involvement in the development and funding of future Internet companies.

 The BRIC nations have over 1 Billion Internet Users combined.

INTERNET CONNECTED WORLD

Enablers will rise that empower users with the ability to extend their reach in to all markets. Foreign Direct Investment will take on a new meaning as investing in foreign companies will be as easy as ordering a sandwich from your favorite local restaurant. Key markets will develop further means of achieving economies of scale by utilizing the Internet to reduce costs and increase revenues. The Internet will further the sharing of information but more importantly will strengthen inter-dependent trade networks, increasing trade between nations. Untapped markets and developing nations will continue to be the engine for the growth of the Internet.

 By 2050, approximately 80 percent of the world will be using the Internet.

INTERNET CONNECTED WORLD

With only 40 percent of the world using the Internet, the bridging of the digital divide will continue to be a goal for tech companies and device developers. The One Laptop Per Child program created by Nicholas Negroponte, has made great strides in creating a low cost laptop that is under $100. Low cost wearable tech devices that will allow access to the Internet, are a future trend for the tech industry. The Internet will feature applications with the ability to control all of your devices and your home appliances. Home automation will make progress in using the Internet for providing real time information to home owners. In addition, confidence in investing in Internet companies will rise as will the understanding that the Internet is growing in to a vital industry for all nations on earth. The Information Age will become a reality as nations that lacked a critical mass of Internet users because of

INTERNET CONNECTED WORLD

affordable access to devices will adopt mainstream methods of promulgating the use of the Internet for business.

 By 2050, all homes will have their systems controlled by a talking computer.

THE FUTURE OF THE INTERNET

The future of the Internet is to empower the way we live and work. There are many that benefit from using the Internet to search for information, sell a product, or speak with family, but the Internet has not fundamentally changed the way we live and work. It has given us greater amusements and made its greatest impact in entertainment. According to the

 Inexpensive computers will assist in bridging the Digital Divide.

INTERNET CONNECTED WORLD

International Telecommunications Union, the number of Internet users increased from 738 million to 3.2 billion in 2015. According to the United Nations, 3 billion people now use the Internet. Considering the population of the Earth is 7 billion, this would mean roughly 40% of the earth is connected to the Internet and 60% is not. Over a few hundred million persons will be coming out of poverty in the 21st century in Asia alone. The Middle Class of India is larger than the entire population of the United States. With the rising of developing nations, the amount of Internet users will increase substantially. The more that first time users utilize the Internet for commerce, the greater the efficiency (cost savings) of the user's operations. This will financially benefit that person as well as create a highly efficient operation.

INTERNET CONNECTED WORLD

 The Internet allows businesses to achieve economies of scale.

Efficient operations replace inefficient ones and greater financial wealth is generated because of it. The Internet is still in its infancy. When the Internet reaches adulthood, it will change the way we live and work. The majority of the world still does not have access to the Internet so bridging the digital divide is a goal that should be reached by 2030. In the future, all people on earth will be online using multiple mobile and Internet applications to access their information in real time. They (the various devices) will provide updates gathered from multiple sources including the user's own mobile phone, in real time. Tools that empower humans will define the future of the Internet. The Internet

INTERNET CONNECTED WORLD

will be a labor saving device as much as it will be an entertainment device.

 By 2050, all interactions between the State and the Citizen will be E-Government digital transactions.

PRIVATE EYES

Will the year 2050 be a freer place for Internet users or will the year 2050 be an online Police State where everything you say is being logged? Is private conversation private when it is online? Do Internet users have a right to privacy when it comes to their own information? Any Internet user would argue that the information that is provided by the user to the website should be not only editable, but also able to be deleted. All information on the Internet is viewed by various security services

INTERNET CONNECTED WORLD

in the nations in which the IP addresses of the websites reside. This is done because the "Deep Internet" which is 500 times larger than the current Internet we use, features criminal organizations that broker in sexual slavery and other various nefarious activities. But to what extent can privacy of users be sacrificed without reducing the privacy of Internet users? That is a subject that has been argued, is being argued currently, and will continue to be argued in the future. There is no agreeable middle ground on what the perfect balance is between security and privacy. It is an unattainable target because barely anyone can agree what the perfect balance is. The best balance is one that favors protecting the privacy of Internet users.

INTERNET CONNECTED WORLD

 The flying car flies like a car and drives like a plan.

FLYING CARS OR AUTOMATED CARS?

Since the 1930's there have been multiple articles written about the future holding flying cars. Today, if your car had fiberglass wings and reached a high enough speed, the force of the lift hitting your wings would cause your car to rise off the ground. In effect you would be flying. A car being able to fly is not Science Fiction and the technology to do it is available now. Then why are not car manufacturers building flying cars? Because they are not in the business of building flying cars. A hybrid car-airplane would most likely drive like a plan and fly like a car. In other words, it would be not the best tool for flying and it would not be the best tool for driving. It would have the worst elements of both car and plane, while denying

INTERNET CONNECTED WORLD

its advantages. Automated cars are a better idea than flying cars; however there is much Research and Development that has not been done to ensure that there are no un-wanted accidents. Car accidents are a major cause of death in the United States and internationally. In an automated car scenario, accidents would be nearly zero. But is not the enjoyment in having a car, being able to drive it? It would be difficult to tell an individual to spend $30,000 on an automobile that they cannot drive. That person would rather keep their money and call a taxi (an automobile they would not be able to drive).

 If people cannot drive a car, they will not buy a car.

The push for automated cars and the eventuality that automated cars will become

the norm, should make automakers and their executives see a future where car sales will go down. Owning a car in the future may be viewed as a luxury, as it is today viewed in Europe.

By 2050, all cars will be automated.

When multiple modes of public transportation exist and cars have become automated personal taxis (in one form or another), then spending $30,000 on a car will become obsolete because cars themselves as we know them will become obsolete. A car is a personal vehicle and without the ability to drive a car, the buyer would not be willing to spend large amounts on it. The benefits are that there will be complete safety on the road and the amount

INTERNET CONNECTED WORLD

of deaths from automobile accidents can possible be reduced to zero.

 By 2050, all your medical records will be online.

INTERNET CONNECTED WORLD

INTERNET CONNECTED MEDICINE

By 2050, your Medical Records will be shared with Governments freely (upon request of course!). Your Medical Records will no longer be private as it will be State managed and controlled. By 2050, all Governments will agree that the medical condition of the Citizen affects the overall health of the nation, and will use your public Medical Records, to assign you the appropriate treatment and prescription drugs. Doctors will no longer be able to add as many prescription drugs as they wish for a patient without some form of regulation from being conducted by the State. This is good for patients and it is bad for Doctors that have made fortunes from bilking poor patients. Also by 2050, Doctors will make lower salaries than they today. Medicine will be Internet based and Internet managed, with minimal interference of a Doctor. The Doctor will be in the role of a

INTERNET CONNECTED WORLD

Case Manager that manages multiple files of patients assigned to him or her.

 By 2050, Doctors will have lower salaries.

GREATER CORPORATE TRANSPARENCY

Publicly traded companies will be more transparent to shareholders with itemized expenses of the corporation available online. Shareholders will be able to vote online for passing measures which the Board of Directors believes to be in the interest of the company. All employees, whether permanent or temporary, will be given an annual review that analyzes the accomplishments and mis-conduct of that employee. Shareholders will be able to vote on an annual basis to remove underperforming employees and to recommend that worthy employees are promoted.

 By 2050, all shareholders will be able to vote online to remove underperforming executives.

By 2050, the Government will rule that up to twenty percent of a corporation, whether private or public, must be held in one form or another by actual customers of that company. In addition, dividends will be mandatory for all public corporations. By 2050, due to globalization, all corporations whether domestic or international, will only have to pay taxes once, rather than facing double or even triple taxation, as many corporations today face. By 2050, all corporations will have a position that will be responsible to

INTERNET CONNECTED WORLD

shareholders and the Government for protecting the environment. This position holder will work to reduce waste, reduce the company's carbon footprint, and produce reports that are submitted to both the Board of Directors as well as the Government body responsible for overseeing it. Protecting the environment will be as important to a corporation in 2050 as is turning a profit.

 By 2050, all corporations will be required to pay dividends.

REAL ESTATE IN 2050

In the future, your standing in society will be based on the building you live in. The building you live in will be a self-contained city that contains all the elements that a city contains including educational institutions, cultural institutions like museums, and natural wildlife habitats.

 By 2050, the building you live in will determine your status in society.

The building will replicate a city in a much smaller version and the building will act as a bank, funding the purchase of units by potential owners that are screened and selected based on their unique skill sets. Your being selected to reside will depend on the skill sets and power in which you bring to the building. The building will have air cleaning mechanisms and air quality defense mechanisms that prevent the introduction of pollution in to its environment. The building you reside in will also use its power and resources to acquire other buildings that can add to their own power.

INTERNET CONNECTED WORLD

By 2050, nearly all humans will live in apartments. Land will become so expensive that very few people will be able to afford it, except in deeply rural areas. The majority of available buildable land will bought by cooperatives, associations, and corporations dedicated to creating "mini-city" type buildings that will determine the status of its inhabitants.

 By 2050, land will be so expensive that only few people will afford it.

WORLD PEACE

By 2050, world peace will break out. The 21st Century will be much safer for humans than the 20th Century was. Why? Because interdependent trade networks between nations creates peace. Commercial trade enables and allows for an atmosphere of peace. 200 million people died in the 20th

INTERNET CONNECTED WORLD

Century from nationalism alone. Nationalism creates nationalistic fervors that can create an atmosphere that is conducive to war and armed conflict. Globalization will create long lasting peace because nations that were previously fighting with weapons are now fighting through trade competition. If War is Business by other means, then business will be the key tool for going to war with rivals, rather than weapons. Heavy expenditures on weapons that will never be used are useless to a nation that is more concerned with job creation, national healthcare, and affordable housing. In the 21st Century, nearly a half a billion individuals will come out of poverty in Brazil, Russia, India, and China. These individuals will want to purchase the same goods and services that are available to individuals in First World nations. Globalization

INTERNET CONNECTED WORLD

will create a safer world, a richer world, and a more interdependent world.

 By 2050, World Peace will break out.

Interdependent trade networks will not only create long lasting peace, but they will also allow for the creation of continental and regional economic alliances, that will greatly benefit its members. Globalization or interdependent trade networks will also allow for a more equitable distribution of wealth. By 2050, the nations that still choose the antiquated method of war and armed conflict in order to pursue their outdated policies, would then face international scrutiny for their obsolete mode of competition.

INTERNET CONNECTED WORLD

 By 2050, Indoor Farming will be the rule, not the exception.

CAN I BORROW A CUP OF CORN?

By 2050, jet airplanes will be fueled primarily by Ethanol or by by-products of other natural fibers. In the movie Back to the Future, Doc uses ordinary trash to fuel his (flying) car. By 2050, your plants and backyard garden will fuel an airplane. Individuals will be able to purchase "Conversion" devices that take natural fibers and create usable fuel, for personal consumption. The devices will be regulated and they will be owned by the State, although they will be assigned to individuals for their private use, based on their consumption. In addition, Urban Farming will become a reality as any building not being used for commercial or residential purposes can be re-assigned for purposes of indoor farming. Efficient indoor farming operations and rooftop farming will be the rule, rather than the exception. Buildings (acting as mini-cities), will also have cooperative indoor farming, where each resident is responsible for the farming operations and its output. The share to be taken by each urban farmer will be equivalent to the amount of time the urban farmer has spent on the urban farm.

 By 2050, Indoor Farming will be the rule, not the exception.

FUTURE OF POLICING

By 2050, the majority of crimes will be solved before any concrete clue is gathered and before the alleged perpetrator is questioned. Information will be so public that everything a human does will be logged and recorded, for further examination in the future. Police will depend on criminals to reveal themselves publicly by way of the Internet, making the search and arrest for criminals easier and less cost intensive.

 By 2050, most crimes will be solved online.

The demand for greater Internet Policing will become prevalent as crimes shift from off-line to online. Identity theft will be the norm and online scammers will use distant locations that are unable to their own local Police, in order to perpetrate the crime. Just as Globalization creates interdependent trade networks, by 2050, there will be interdependent criminal networks. They will use the Internet to liaison and to plan their next activity. Police will, in the future, put their focus on Internet crimes, as blue collar crimes will be reduced to nearly

INTERNET CONNECTED WORLD

zero. Additionally, more laws will be passed as to the consequences of Internet crime, but the laws passed will be for White Collar crime rather than Blue Collar crime. By 2050, White Collar crimes will be dealt with more severely than Blue Collar crime. There will be two standards for criminals (blue collar and white collar) and this will prompt social justice activists to question whether such a differentiation is justified. In addition, Police will not be able to detain anyone for any reason, without some form of permit, provided by a judge. The majority of policing in the future will be conducted using electronic intelligence, online and offline, reducing the amount of casualties suffered by Police Officers during their application of the law.

INTERNET CONNECTED WORLD

 By 2050, most crimes will be solved online.

Cameras with facial recognition software will be the main tool for Police forces to identify and locate criminals, meaning there will be a reduction in police forces in the streets. The facial recognition software, will allow for cross-referencing of databases and pattern recognition, making criminals in to walking Police targets for arrest. This will reduce the burden on over-worked Police officers and will make catching criminals an automated job.

 By 2050, the majority of crimes will be coordinated online.

INTERNET CONNECTED WORLD

EDUCATION IN 2050
In the future, education will be 100 percent in the form of hologram teachers or video screens, that will be have AI capability. It will be online and used off-line in classrooms. These AI or Artificial Intelligence teachers will teach at all levels. This will save, potentially billions of dollars, every years for the State. Educators will not lose their positions because of this. Educators will be the ones teaching on the video screens and in the form of AI hologram teachers.

 By 2050, all education will be video based and online.

Educators will be able to more comfortably conduct their jobs, which is research. By having more time to conduct research, Professors and teachers at all levels, will be able to have more time for organizing, preparing, and researching. The content will be created and distributed by the educator. Using holographic projectors or even ultra slim wall sized televisions, the experience would not really be any different than having an actual educator in front of you. The educator could even, using remote viewing technology like cameras with the addition of a camera, could monitor the class and answer a student's question. The amount of money that will be saved using this system will allow the money to be used for essential student services like having a 24 hour library, providing subsidized meals to students, and discounted parking. For those educators that will be angered by this, they must understand, they are not losing their jobs! And education in a capitalist system is a commercial function of the economy. Many times, individuals that spent large amounts of money to receive a standard Bachelor's

INTERNET CONNECTED WORLD

Degree, cannot find a job, making them have to seek work in other fields. Luckily, the Internet in 2050, will be one that will create new positions that do not currently exist. By 2050, the majority of the developed nations on earth, will depend on their Internet small businesses to generate essential tax revenue and to assist in the growth of the Gross Domestic Product (GDP). Internet small business will be the number driver of job growth and job creation in 2050.

 By 2050, most crimes will be solved online.

INTERNET CONNECTED WORLD

THE LAST WORD

The future will be a much more different place than the one we reside in. It will be safer, cleaner, and more efficient, than it is today. In the future, the people you associate with will be more important to you than your nuclear or extended family. Humans will be less cautious of each other because by 2050, society will have enabled the proper regulations to stop individuals from causing economic and bodily harm to each other. The future will be a safer future because there will be less homeless, less armed conflict, and less un-employed. By 2050, the need for weapons will be outdated, as humans use the mode of business to compete with one another. The future will be an Internet based one where economies of scale will be reached enabling companies to save vital funds for growth.

Sincerely,
Kambiz Mostofizadeh

INTERNET CONNECTED WORLD

INDEX

INTERNET CONNECTED WORLD

NOTES

INTERNET CONNECTED WORLD

NOTES

INTERNET CONNECTED WORLD

NOTES

INTERNET CONNECTED WORLD

NOTES

INTERNET CONNECTED WORLD

NOTES

INTERNET CONNECTED WORLD

NOTES

INTERNET CONNECTED WORLD

NOTES

INTERNET CONNECTED WORLD

NOTES

INTERNET CONNECTED WORLD

NOTES

INTERNET CONNECTED WORLD

NOTES

INTERNET CONNECTED WORLD

NOTES

www.ingramcontent.com/pod-product-compliance
Lightning Source LLC
LaVergne TN
LVHW022323060326

832902LV00020B/3640